IS YOUR CHILD WIRED FOR SUCCESS?

THE INCONTESTABLE TRUTH
ABOUT ACHIEVEMENT

DAN LIER

Including
The Psycho-Success Developmental Theory

IS YOUR CHILD WIRED FOR SUCCESS

Dan Lier

CONTENTS

INTRODUCTION

W hat allows people to become successful? When people meet someone who has achieved noteworthy success, it's human nature to be curious how they did it.

> *"All human's by nature have
> the desire to know" - Aristotle*

What made them successful?

What special skills do they have?

Were they just "blessed" or do they have a certain "something" which allows them to uncover success?

Can I do the same?

These common questions have been asked for years; most likely for hundreds of years. In my keynote talks and trainings, both domestically and internationally, people always want the

1

answer to the question of what it takes to be successful.

I've been in the business of achievement and productivity for over 20 years and based on my conversations with people, there is no shortage for answers and opinions for what makes people successful.

The Short Story

I earned my Masters degree in 1986 and became intrigued with personal achievement and the psychology that separates those who make it happen, from those who don't. I embarked on a near 30-year study of human behavior.

Originally I was focused on sports performance, as I was coaching college basketball and had just completed playing five years of college eligibility as a player and winning two straight national titles.

As a player, how did our team find the resources to win back-to-back national titles? There were multiple games down the stretch that could have gone either way, yet how did we find a way to win?

There were teams that could have been more talented than our team, yet we found a way to win when it counted.

That's really what it's about... how to gather the resources to perform at the level necessary to achieve the result you desire.

Later, as a college basketball coach, I found it fascinating how often times players who had less talent, worked harder than players who were blessed with pure athletic ability. The more athletically talented players often times took short-cuts thus didn't maximize their true potential. Then of course, there are the rare basketball players that are familiar to the American culture, such as Jordan, LeBron, Kobe, Magic & Bird to name a few, who were blessed with the talent, and yet possessed the proper mindset and work ethic to rise above the competition and create a separation.

This simple equation holds true outside the world of sports as well. It holds true in business, in entertainment and as an entrepreneur.

Shortly after my college basketball playing and coaching experience, I found myself in the corporate world selling commercial insurance. During my training program, I was introduced Denis Waitley via audiotapes, one of the leaders in personal achievement in the late 80's. Denis was a psychologist who's 1979 best selling book "The Psychology of Winning" started me on the path of discovery. A discovery to understand

3

human achievement and what gives some people the ability to do what it takes to win.

I was intrigued with the possibility that a person's psychology would, or could dictate a person's success or failure. I studied most advanced thinkers and philosophers, such as James Allen, Wallace Wattles, Napoleon Hill and Zig Ziglar. One by one, I studied, I learned and I applied. I listened and took notes to hours of audio by Brian Tracy and Tony Robbins. In Tony Robbins' first book "Unlimited Power" I became intrigued with NLP and how language patterns affect how people hear things thus affecting what they do. As I result, researched and learned about Richard Bandler and John Grinder, the founders of NLP.

In 1996 and I went to Kona, Hawaii and earned my certification in NLP by Tad James. Tad is considered one of the best NLP masters in the world. My acquisition of NLP knowledge took my skills to the next level. In addition, I was fortunate to work with Tony Robbins for six years, which placed me an environment of constant learning, coaching, presenting and growing. I was performing corporate talks and coaching business executives everyday. Most interesting to me was seeing and experiencing the differences in human behavior first hand.

Tony Robbins' company was RRI (Robbins Research International), and one of my positions was titled FSR (field sales representative). I was giving success presentations two and three times a day with the goal to sell tickets to Tony Robbins' 1-day business event. I was on 100% commission, so selling tickets was the ultimate goal. The meetings had anywhere from 5 people to 100's of people in attendance, yet most were in the 10 – 30 people range. When it came time for the close, meaning asking for a commitment from the people in the room to go to the event, it was fascinating to see how people responded in front of one another.

Typically, people associate a selling situation where it's one–on-one, or maybe one with two, meaning a sales person and a couple. My experience was different.

With 30 people in the room, human behavior changes. I was highly skilled in closing and I understood human behavior, so after a series of pre-frames, reframes and a test close, I would close for the sale in front of the entire the group. With skill and with precision, I would address each person one by one in front of the group and look to uncover the "excuse" and give them the logic, reason and emotion to sign-up, commit and attend the event. It was incredible training for me.

As a natural progression, I studied what I consider to be the most influential behavioral psychologists in the world and based my writings, teachings and video releases on their work. People such as:

- William James
- Sigmund Freud
- Carl Rogers
- Albert Bandura
- Jean Piaget
- Ivan Pavlov
- Kurt Lewin
- Erik Erikson
- B.F. Skinner
- Viktor Frankl
- Carl Jung
- John Watson

These twelve psychologists laid my foundation of behavioral psychology today and represent the fundamentals of the science of psychology. The more I studied this group of men, the more I realized how significant their research was and how <u>human behavior is predictable</u>.

Can people really be wired for success?

Yes we can. Through my research, studies and professional experiences with hundreds and hundreds of clients, acquaintances and personal relationships, I've uncovered the foundation and the basis for the "success wiring" that impacts the advancement of humans.

In this book I'm going cover three areas:

1. Present my theory on how people are wired for success… or how they are wired to be "average" or even an underachiever.

2. Share personal stories of other people who have the success wiring.

3. How our "wiring" impacts our intimate relationships.

1

WHAT IS THE KEY TO SUCCESS?

What is the Key to Success?

People often ask me, "What's the key to success? It happens at least once a month. Most often after a corporate keynote talk or a training. It doesn't matter where the location of the talk is… California, New York, Colorado, Venice, Istanbul or Copenhagen; people want to know… "What's the key to success?"

It's a good question, and who wouldn't want to know the key to success? What happens next is the person who just asked me the question starts sharing their take on the key to success. The most popular unsolicited responses from people are as follows:

- Hard Work
- Knowing the Right People
- Handling Rejection
- Drive
- Goal Setting
- Time Management
- Communication Skills
- Continued Development
- Attitude
- Staying Focused
- Clarity of Vision
- Discipline

These are all great answers, and can be applicable to people all over the world. As a matter of fact, let's take a look at Napoleon Hill's first book, **The Law of Success** published in 1928. The Law of Success was revolutionary in its time. Initially, Napoleon Hill traveled around the country and delivered the message as a lecture to people who wanted to find success.

The table of contents to The Law of Success in 16 Lessons:

1. The Master Mind
2. Definite Chief Aim
3. Self-Confidence
4. The Habit of Saving
5. Initiative and Leadership
6. Imagination
7. Enthusiasm
8. Self-Control
9. The Habit of Doing More than Paid For
10. A Pleasing Personality
11. Accurate Thinking
12. Concentration
13. Cooperation
14. Profiting by Failure
15. Tolerance
16. The Golden Rule

Napoleon Hill's research and writing was directed and funded by Andrew Carnegie, who was one of the wealthiest and most successful men of the time.

Napoleon Hill interviewed over 100 American millionaires such as J.P. Morgan, John D. Rockefeller, Thomas Edison, Henry Ford and Alexander Graham Bell. These names are the equivalent of Donald Trump, Oprah Winfrey, Steve Jobs and Warren Buffett of the current times.

It was interesting that Andrew Carnegie funded and directed Napoleon Hill's research, as Carnegie himself was a true rags-to-riches story.

"Success" as a destination, has been talked about for years.

How do I get there?

What makes people successful?

Napoleon Hill gave lectures to people about his findings in the late 1920's, and today in 2015, people are still asking the same questions.

This endless search from those before me lit a fire within me that has burned for close to 30 years. I've studied the most respected success and business strategists', the most impactful psychologists in the history of our world, and conducted my own study of over 300 subjects over a 20-year period. As a result, I developed the Psycho-Success Developmental Theory.

The Psycho-Success Developmental Theory is a blueprint for success. There are many factors, situations and circumstances associated with success, yet the Psycho-Success Developmental Theory is the first of its kind, structured look at "HOW" the success wiring is developed in human beings.

In the following chapter, I'm going to share with you my theory, then provide examples of people who have shown the theory to be true.

2

PSYCHO-SUCCESS DEVELOPMENTAL THEORY

Psycho-Success Development Theory

German-born American Psychologist Erik Erikson's theory of Psycho-Social development indicates human personality develops through eight stages of development, and their personality is impacted by social experiences through the course of one's life. Austria's Sigmund Freud's theory on psycho-sexual development indicates human development is impacted through five stages based on their sexual urges and sexual drive. My research indicates there is a development process for "success principles," or as some would say, the ingredients for success.

If psychologist and behaviorist B.F. Skinner can teach, or some would say "condition" pigeons to turn in a circle based on showing the pigeon the word "turn" and reinforcing that behavior, it's evident that behavior is a learned skill and shaped by our environment. It is my conclusion that we as humans, are "wired for success" or "wired for failure" based on our developmental experiences starting at a young age. The fact is we don't just get wired for success or failure, as that sounds a bit harsh. Humans get wired to be "one of the pack," to "just fit in," or even "mediocrity."

B.F. Skinner was an extreme behaviorist who believed that free-will as a human was an illusion. He believed that all human actions were the result of the consequences of that same action. Similar to Albert Bandura (Social Learning Theory), Kurt Lewin (the founder of social psychology) and Erik Erikson (Theory on psychosocial development), my findings indicate human behavior is impacted and shaped by multiple factors.

With that being said, the foundation for human or animal behavior is a response to events in the environment. What a person (or any organism for that matter) has to do, is survive in the real, physical world. It does this by behaving in response to the challenges presented by that world.

My 30 years of research and my decade long "Success Project" indicates that the components necessary for success are predictable based on how a child was raised, and his/her exposure to various environmental opportunities and situational leadership.

I worked personally with hundreds and hundreds of clients over the years in a "Rogerian Therapy" and psychoanalytic style of coaching and communicating. My "Success Project" was a decade long study of over 300 individuals, both men and women. I studied their current state of achievement and fulfillment, their upbringing and guidance, whether that upbringing was from a parent or a primary caregiver. As a result, I developed the theory on psycho-success development.

The psycho-success development theory is a model that shows how, where and why the "success wiring" is either developed or undeveloped.

As an expert in human behavior, I realize that all people have the desire to be the "best they can be." Generally speaking, people have the desire to improve their lives. As a highly trained and seasoned success coach, when working with a client, my goal has always been:

1. Where do you want to go?
2. How are you going to get there?

Always forward focused, yet curious about why the client feels "stuck" or ill prepared to succeed, I ask a series of strategic questions about the clients' developmental years. What I found was fascinating. The results of the questions formatted my theory on psycho-success development, or in everyday terms, developing the proper "mental wiring" to achieve success. As a result I gathered the research and information and wrote this book titled "Is Your Child Wired for Success – The incontestable truth about achievement"

3

PSYCHO-SUCCESS DEVELOPMENTAL THEORY

(Outline)

Psycho-Success Developmental Theory

(Outline)

<u>Pre-Developmental Stage (0-2)</u>

"Loving Parents," express their love in two methods:

- "Teaching" Parent
- "Coddling – Enabling" parent

Test Example: Do you let the child "cry-out" or do you bring them in your bed?

<u>Foundational Stage (3-10 yrs)</u> - ends approx 3rd grade

Two Planes of learning:

1. How to Act: (from primary caretaker and role models)

- Based on Bandera's Social Learning theory, which is based on Observational Learning, Modeling & Imitation
- From Siblings, other children, TV shows & school

2. How to Be:

- From Primary Caregiver

How primary Caregivers handle:

- Frustration
- Failure
- Success
- Relationships
- Anger
- Do they lie on the couch all day?
- Are they motivated, and upbeat?

Foundational Stage Learnings:

R-ules
C-oncequeces
R-espect
I-dentity
S-elf Esteem
S-elf Image

3. What is Possible –
Much in the form of Language

(What they learn from primary caregivers)

a. What is Possible For Themselves

- You can do it
- You're amazing
- You're a hard worker
- You'll never be anything
- You can't do anything right

b. What is Possible In the World

- The world is your oyster
- Good things happen
- Opportunities are everywhere
- Government holds you down
- No opportunities
- Too expensive
- The system is corrupt
- Anything is possible

Hard Wiring Stage (11-18 yrs)

- Rules – Structure
- Consequences
- Work-Reward Relationship
- Quality of Work
- Drive for More / Drive to Sustain
- Overcoming Obstacles / Perseverance
- Recovery Time

Two Guiding Beliefs

1. Who am I (self-image)
2. What's necessary to succeed?

4

HOW THE WIRING HAPPENS

"How the Wiring Happens"

Psycho-Success Development Theory

Pre-Development Stage (birth to 2 yrs)

During the pre-development stage, the child is exploring and learning both in body, the relationship with space and the experience of love. Love and trust as well as mistrust has an effect on the child's development, yet shows limited impact on the overall "life-success" as an adult. This stage could also be titled the Parental Development Stage. Parents in general, especially "first-time" parents are formulating their boundaries and how they should "parent."

One factor which develops during the pre-development stage (PDS) is the parent's response to the child's needs, which is termed the "parent-response" factor. During the PDS, when the child is in need, because communication skills are not developed at this stage, the child typically cries or screams.

An example that all parents can relate with is when the parents decide it's time for the baby to sleep in his or her own crib in a different room. Even with audio and video monitors, this process is still very challenging and unnerving to many parents. If you've been a parent, you know this feeling oh so well.

The parents place the baby in his or her crib in the separate room and they walk out gingerly. Some parents can't bear to actually shut the door, so they leave it cracked in order to have a view of the baby in the crib. We all have a solid idea of what happens next... the baby cries.

"Oh the poor child," one mother shared with me. "He is alone for the first time." Does he feel abandoned? Is he afraid? Does he feel not loved? And the gut-wrenching feeling of all this questions run through the minds of many parents during this pre-development stage milestone.

Some parents let the child cry themselves out and fall to sleep, while other parents are not able to let the child cry and respond by picking up the baby. In this example, the parents who let the child cry themselves out and fall to sleep have a lower parent-response factor, whereas the parents' who felt it necessary to "rescue" the child, have a higher parent-response ratio.

The individual child learns in the Pre-Development Stage if his caretakers will respond when he/she cries or screams. In essence the child is learning his/her sense of boundaries as to what level their parents will be there for them through life development.

Having a high or low parent response factor is not a determining factor in whether the child will be wired for success or not. The challenge lies with the parents who may carry out this same behavior through the two following stages of development, which are the foundational stage and the hard-wiring stage.

Coming to "rescue" your child when they are in need is a natural and healthy response for a parent. Yet, not lowering the parent – response factor as the child matures is a problem. Ironically parents that feel "they care the most" often times become a "**success inhibitor**."

Parents who maintain a high parent-response factor become a hindrance to the child's success development. My findings indicate parents with low self-esteem, insecurity or those who have faced emotional distress, tend to carry out a high parent-response factor through the child's next two stages of development. Unfortunately, a high parent-response factor during stage two and three of the psycho-success developmental theory, will impact the child in a negative manner in their success wiring.

I've identified the two types of parents in the Pre-Development stage as

1. Loving "Codling" parents
2. Loving "Teaching" parents

The generalization made here in the first stage of the Psycho-Success Developmental theory is that all children are loved. We know that fact is not true, yet for sake of creating two specific parental patterns, we are making a generalization all babies are loved. Opening up the theory to how many babies are not loved, or why they are not loved, opens up an entirely subjective study. Maybe for another time.

5

FOUNDATIONAL
STAGE

Foundational Stage (Age 3-10)

Age 3-10 years is the period of time where the child develops the foundational tools that will lead to success or mediocrity.

The foundational stage of the child is profoundly impacted by parental philosophies of the primary caregivers. For clarity, when using the term primary caregivers, I am referring to the adult(s) who spends the most time with the child. Most often I am referring to the parents, yet because each child could be faced with a unique situation, the term primary caregiver also may refer to:

- Step-parents
- Nannies
- Family members other than parents

- Foster home situations
- Alternate family

We've all seen nannies, uncles or other families who spend more time with the kids than the actual parents.

Note: sometimes this is a good thing. Parents who aren't present have been described by some as equivalent to "no parents at all."

Who are the children learning from? Who is laying down the foundation for the "success wiring" for the developing child?

The primary caregivers shape and develop the "success wiring" for the child as they experience the world.

Introduction to Rules & Consequences

Children who have a concrete understanding of rules and consequences formulate decisions that would be considered "good choices," thus advancing the child in the direction of success.

Consequences, or the "if-then" equation are learned from primary caregivers. The adults in the relationship literally form the child's understanding of how the world functions.

When a child reaches to touch the hot fire or element on the stove, the consequence is immediate and non-negotiable. The hot element or fire burns the child's skin. As a result, the child understands the relationship between fire and his/her body. Fire = pain. The child's behavior is modified. Simple equation.

When a child behaves in a manner that would be considered inappropriate and the primary caregiver provides no consequences for that behavior, the behavior is then accepted as a behavior that can be replicated, and of course repeated. This pattern for formulation starts at approximately age 3 and has tremendous life-long impact on the child's understanding of foundational rules, which are present throughout the life of the child.

5-Year Old James

In the most elementary fashion, the primary care giver is shaping the child's behavior based on their response to the behavior. For example, a 5-year old boy named James has a tendency to hit his mother with his fist in a punching motion.

James is 5 years old. It would be irrational to make a statement that James is a bad kid or that James is violent. He's only 5. Maybe James has been exposed to aggressive forms of behavior in person or on television, or maybe James simply has an extraordinary amount of energy.

Nevertheless, James punches his mom in the face and neck area when she picks him up. We've all seen this situation play out with adults and children whether is be at a grocery store, a birthday party or at an amusement park. It happens.

How James' mother responds to his hitting and punching determines how James is "wired" for the specific behavior of hitting, as well as future situations.

Let go back to the fire example. Imagine if a young child touches the hot stove, yet there is no response of immediate pain, one would estimate the child would touch the hot stove again. What if the parent knew consistent exposure via touch to the hot stove would lead to health problems when the child was 16. Do you think the parent or primary caretaker would provide consequences so the "unknowing" child wouldn't cause themselves pain or health issues in the future? I would suggest they would indeed.

Thus, therein lies the danger in James' mother not responding to his hitting or punching with a response that indicates to James the behavior is not acceptable. At age 5, James doesn't understand hitting someone, especially someone you are supposed to respect, is not culturally accepted. If not changed, this behavior will cause

James to have issues, challenges and setbacks in his adult life.

Consequences

When the primary caregiver does not follow-through with consequences, often times as a result of the primary caregivers lack of knowledge or lack of confidence, the child is developing a reference for the structure of events dealing with behavior. Often times the primary caregiver feels guilt for "punishing" or reprimanding the child, yet ironically the primary caregiver is programming the child for mediocrity or failure.

During this foundation stage, the child learns the concept of "rules" or lack thereof. As adults, we live in a culture governed by rules and consequences.

To be successful in the system in which we live, a person must operate within certain rules. The child's understanding of the importance of rules, are formulated from the primary caregiver during the impactful foundational stage.

Because we live in a world where business success can be reached non-traditionally, many rules have changed, i.e. Steve Jobs (Apple), Mark Zuckerberg (FaceBook) and Palmer Luckey (Oculus). Just as they were in the times of

Andrew Carnegie, the foundational keys necessary to achieve success still remain consistent today, as they always will.

The Foundational stage during psycho-success development consists of Three facets of learning which impact their future success:

1. How to Act
2. How to Be
3. Belief – Based Primarily on Language

6

"HOW TO ACT"

Foundational Stage

How to Act

Foundational Stage

1. **How to Act** is impacted by three methods:

   a) Observational Learning
   b) Modeling
   c) Imitation

All of which support and are components of psychologist Albert Bandura's Social Learning theory.

Bandura's 1961 "Bobo Doll Experiment" was a game-changer in respect to children learning by observing.

Young children in the foundational stage are learning How to Act by observing, modeling and imitating, and they do so primarily in the following areas:

   • Other children at school
   • Their siblings
   • What they observe on television/internet
   • Their parents/family or primary caregivers

Children in the Foundational Stage are essentially learning "How to Act" by what they experience in their environment. It would make sense that a child who grew up in an environment where both parents were present and graduated from an Ivy League school and were members of numerous high-society social clubs would have a difference sense of how he or she should ACT verses a child who goes through the Foundational stage with parents who may be struggling financially, struggling through personal issues, addictions and self-esteem issues.

The Bobo Doll Experient 1961[1]

The participants in this experiment were 36 boys and 36 girls from the Stanford University nursery school. All children were between the ages of 42 months and 71 months. The children were organized into 4 groups and a control group. 24 children were exposed to an aggressive model and 24 children were exposed to a non-aggressive model. The two groups were then divided into males and females, which ensured that half of the children were exposed to models of their own sex and the other half were exposed to models of the opposite sex. The remaining 24 children were part of a control group.

For the experiment, each child was exposed to the scenario individually, so as not to be influenced or distracted by classmates. The first part of the experiment involved bringing a child and the adult model into a playroom. In the playroom, the child was seated in one corner filled with highly appealing activities such as stickers and stamps. The adult model was seated in another corner containing a toy set, a mallet, and an inflatable Bobo doll.

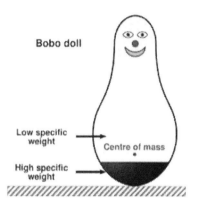

Before leaving the room, the experimenter explained to the child that the toys in the adult corner were only for the adult to play with.

During the aggressive model scenario, the adult would begin by playing with the toys for approximately one minute. After this time the adult would start to show aggression towards the Bobo doll. Examples of this included hitting/punching the Bobo doll and using the toy mallet to hit the Bobo doll in the face. The aggressive model would also verbally assault the

Bobo doll yelling "Sock him," "Hit him down," "Kick him," "Throw him in the air," or "Pow". After a period of about 10 minutes, the experimenter came back into the room, dismissed the adult model, and took the child into another playroom. The non-aggressive adult model simply played with the other toys for the entire 10 minute-period. In this situation, the Bobo doll was completely ignored by the model, then the child was taken out of the room.

The next stage of the experiment, took place with the child and experimenter in another room filled with interesting toys such as trucks, dolls, and a spinning top. The child was invited to play with them. After about 2 minutes the experimenter decides that the child is no longer allowed to play with the toys, explaining that she is reserving those toys for the other children. This was done to build up frustration in the child. The experimenter said that the child could instead play with the toys in the experimental room (this included both aggressive and non-aggressive toys). In the experimental room the child was allowed to play for the duration of 20 minutes while the experimenter evaluated the child's play.

The first measure recorded was based on physical aggression such as punching, kicking, sitting on the Bobo doll, hitting it with a mallet, and tossing it around the room. Verbal aggression was the second measure recorded. The judges counted each time the children imitated the aggressive adult model and recorded their results. The third measure was the number of times the mallet was used to display other forms of aggression than hitting the doll. The final measure included modes of aggression shown by the child that were not direct imitation of the role-model's behavior (Bandura, Ross & Ross 1961).[2]

The Images below are actual images from Bandura's 1961 Bobo Doll Experiment:

Boy with Hammer

Boy with Gun

Results

Bandura found the children exposed to the aggressive model were more likely to act in physically aggressive ways than those who were not exposed to the aggressive model. For those children exposed to the aggressive model, the number of imitative physical aggressions exhibited by the boys was 38.2 and 12.7 for the girls.[3] The results concerning gender differences strongly supported Bandura's prediction that children are more influenced by same-sex models. Results also showed that boys exhibited more aggression when exposed to aggressive male models than boys exposed to aggressive female models. When exposed to aggressive male models, the number of aggressive instances exhibited by boys averaged 104 compared to 48.4 aggressive instances exhibited by boys who were exposed to aggressive female models.

While the results for the girls show similar findings, the results were less drastic. When exposed to aggressive female models, the number of aggressive instances exhibited by girls averaged 57.7 compared to 36.3 aggressive instances exhibited by girls who were exposed to aggressive male models.

Bandura also found that the children exposed to the aggressive model were more likely to act in verbally aggressive ways than those who were not exposed to the aggressive model. The number of imitative verbal aggressions exhibited by the boys was 17 times and 15.7 times by the girls (Hock 2009: 89). In addition, the results indicated that the boys and girls who observed the non-aggressive model exhibited far less non-imitative mallet aggression than in the control group, which had no model.

The experimenters concluded that observing adult behavior influences a child to think that this type of behavior is acceptable, thus weakening the child's aggressive inhibitions. Reduced aggressive inhibitions in children means that they are more likely to respond to future situations with more aggression.

Lastly, the evidence strongly supports that males tend to be more aggressive than females. When all instances of aggression are tallied, males exhibited 270 aggressive instances compared to 128 aggressive instances exhibited by females.[4]

7

"HOW TO BE"

Foundational Stage

Foundational Stage

The second segment of the foundational stage is "How to Be"

2. How to Be

The segment of "**How to Be**" is impacted by the primary care giver, which again could be any or all of the following:

- Parents
- Family members (uncle, aunt, etc)
- Nanny
- Foster Home
- Juvenile Program

During the Foundational Stage of Psycho-Success development, children are learning "How to Be" adults from their role models, which are the people who are around them the most. Watching the primary caregivers (which obviously could be the parent or parents) handle situations, respond to challenges, discipline, blame, find solutions and treat loved ones leaves an imprint on the young child for success or failure.

"How to Be" in the foundation stage, touches multiple areas of developing patterns of dealing with the physical world. Understand that a young boy who observes his father yelling at his mother learns the behavior is appropriate and will often times follow-suit.

A young boy who observes his father treating his wife as if she were a treasure, will in fact have the tendency to treat women is his life with love and respect.

A young boy who may observe his father sitting on the couch complaining about lack of opportunity rather than hustling everyday to create opportunity, learns specific behavior for dealing with challenges.

A young boy who observes a passive father and a dominant mother will assume that he as a man should act the same.

A young boy or girl who observes domestic abuse from father to mother or mother to father, either physically or emotionally, will make the assumption the specific behavior is acceptable. With the recent NFL issues in regards to domestic abuse and child abuse, Observational Learning has become a key focus for changing behavior of the next generation. Adrian Peterson experienced "How to Be" from his father in the foundation stage of pycho-success development as indicated by his statements on the subject.

During this specific segment, the child is developing an understanding of 5 important keys to success, all of which have no relationship to the financial position or educational level of the parents or primary caretakers.

1. Rules
2. Consequences
3. Respect
4. Self-Image
5. Identity

The 5 Keys of Success During the Foundational Stage

1. Rules

Rules are part of existence in our world. It is cliché' to say that rules are made to be broken. A popular saying for some, yet to succeed in the world we must have an understanding and respect of rules.

- A financial advisor who doesn't follow the rules, ends up in prison.
- A college student who doesn't follow rules ends up getting expelled, flunking out, or both.
- A college athlete who doesn't follow the rules loses his or her scholarship.
- The employee who doesn't arrive to work at the predetermined and agreed upon time

ends up getting fired and looking for another job.

- When a person decides they want to be in the profession of selling, there are rules.
- When you decide to play any "game," there are always rules.
- When a person decides to pursue or be a part of any organization, corporation or movement, there are rules in place.

The understanding and respect of rules are paramount in the foundational stage. "Pushing or bending" the rules is a trait carried by high-achieving entrepreneurs. On the other hand, breaking the rules leads to failure and loss; emotionally, physically and financially – See Lance Armstrong, Bernie Madov and disgraced senator John Edwards to name a few.

2. Consequences

Consequences are the concrete slab to the building; they are the bricks and mortar for the foundational stage. Consequences shape the behavior of the developing child. In the earlier example, the touching of the fire, and of course fire resulting in pain is the elementary yet clear example of consequences.

As mature adults, we have come to the conclusion that there are consequences for every action, both positive consequences and negative consequences. The behaviorist would refer to consequences at reinforcement. All of us, even to this day are being reinforced on a daily basis, it's just about who is going to do it better.

"I Can Shape your Child"

John Watson was considered in expert in child rearing during the late 1920's and 1930's. In his book "Psychological Care of the Infant and Child (1928)," Watson described child rearing as a science, a science based in part of his research and development at John Hopkins University. Watson's work was well respected and influenced other authors, such as Benjamin Spock. Spock's 1946 publication "Baby and Child Care" was the second best-selling book next to the Bible.

John B. Watson, an American psychologist who established the psychological school of behaviorism shared his views on the impact of environment for a developing child:

"Give me a dozen healthy infants, well-formed, and my own specified world to bring them up in and I'll guarantee to take any one at random and train him to become any type of specialist I might select – doctor, lawyer, artist, merchant-chief and, yes, even beggar-man and thief, regardless of his talents, penchants, tendencies, abilities, vocations, and race of his ancestors. I am going beyond my facts and I admit it, but so have the advocates of the contrary and they have been doing it for many thousands of years.[5]

Consequences shape behavior, as does a lack of consequences.

3. Respect

The definition of respect is to admire (someone or something) deeply, as a result of their abilities, qualities, or achievements. Respect is earned it is not given. A parent does not automatically have respect from a child just because they are the "parents." In my 20+ years working with people, I've encountered many financially successful people that don't have the respect of their children. Parents who don't follow-through with consequences and discipline earn a lower level of respect from their children.

As I interviewed over 300 parents over a 10-year period, the parents who were concerned with "being liked" by their children earned far less respect from their children than the parents who were not concerned about "being liked." Ironically, parents who implemented rules with consequences (within reasonable boundaries of course) earned the respect from their children, all the while giving their kids the gift of understanding of what it takes to be successful as a human being in our culture.

Respecting someone because they are older is about as logical as sending a piece of mail through the U.S. mail system when you need it there overnight. It doesn't make sense. Respect comes from someone who walks their talk; someone who does what they say they are going to do.

When a parent makes a statement in a moment of frustration, such as "ok, that's it, no X-box for you for a week" – yet they child ends up playing for hours that same evening, the parent is teaching the child that their word means nothing - I don't follow through on my word. There is nothing positive about this specific pattern.

Below are examples of potential deductions, which evolve into beliefs for the young person moving from the foundational stage to the "hard wiring stage" based on what they encountered from the primary care taker during the foundational stage:

- I don't have to listen to anyone... they never follow through.
- Oh, I do have to listen to my friends parents Mr. Jones or Mrs. Smith or I have a negative experience.

- I respect Mr. Jones and Mrs. Smith.
- I don't respect my mom. She doesn't follow-through. I love her, yet I don't respect her.
- My parents are pushovers.
- My parents are strict. - Often times during the foundational stage, being strict simply means having rules and consequences along with those rules. Interesting how strict has a negative connotation from young people, yet those who encounter rules and consequences typically have a clearer understanding of what it takes to be successful.
- The people around me don't care about me. - Children who have no rules and consequences often times look for someone or something to belong to. Someone who shows an interest.

4. Self-Image

Self-image is the personal view, or mental picture that we have of ourselves. Self-image is an internal dictionary that describes the characteristics of the self, including beliefs as intelligent, beautiful, ugly, talented, selfish, and kind. These characteristics form a collective representation of our assets and liabilities as we see them.

<u>Self-image is a product of learning</u>. Parents and caregivers significantly influence our self-image during the foundational stage of Psycho-Success Development. Parents and caregivers are mirrors reflecting back to us an image of ourselves.

Our experiences with others such as teachers, friends and family add to the image in the mirror. Relationships reinforce what we think and feel about ourselves.

The image we see in the mirror may be a real or distorted view of who we really are. Based on this view, we develop either a positive or a negative self-image. The strengths and weaknesses we have internalized affect how we act today. We continually take in information and evaluate ourselves in multiple domains such as physical appearance (How do I look?), performance (How am I doing?), and relationships (How important am I?).

With a positive self-image, we recognize and own our assets and potentials while being realistic about our liabilities and limitations.

With a negative self-image, we focus on our faults and weaknesses, distorting failure and imperfections.

Self-image is important because how we think about ourselves affects how we feel about ourselves and how we interact with others and the world around us. A positive self-image can enhance our physical, mental, social, emotional, and spiritual well-being. Conversely, a negative self-image can decrease our satisfaction and ability to function in these areas.

5. Personal Identity

Personal identity is the concept you develop about yourself that evolves over the course of your life. This may include aspects of your life that you have no control over, such as where you grew up or the color of your skin. Personal identity also is developed by the choices you make in life, such as how you spend your time and what you believe. You demonstrate portions of your personal identity outwardly through what you wear and how you interact with other people. You may also keep some elements of your personal identity to yourself, even when these parts of yourself are very important.

Have you ever struggled with the question, 'Who am I?' or thought about who you might become in the future? These questions have been thought about and discussed throughout history, in particular by philosophers who have immersed themselves in the search for knowledge about the nature of being human. Such questions as 'What does it mean to be a person?' and 'Do I matter?' have engaged key thinkers and created conversations that we still grapple with in our society.

Most people feel they want to endure in some way, both in their lives and beyond death. The philosophy of personal identity aims to address these matters of existence and how we even know we exist through time.

Initially we develop our personal identity from our experiences and interactions with our direct environment - our parents and/or primary caregivers. **In the foundational stage of Psycho-Success development, our personal identity is impacted by our experiences and feelings of achievement, love and acceptance**. If the child is loved, accepted and feels safe, they develop a positive identity – and identity of possibilities.

A child who is develops in an environment without sensory experiences of love, acceptance and achievement, develops a very limited, non-meaningful identity.

The experiences of love, acceptance and achievement would seem to infer constant praise and unconditional love, yet what must be noted here, is an environment of love, acceptance and achievement is one containing rules and consequences, along with love and acceptance. Without the rules, consequences and respect, the child has a limited understanding of what it takes to be successful, thus their personal identity is limited.

8

MORE ABOUT
JOHN B. WATSON

More about John B. Watson:

John B. Watson was one of the most interesting figures in the modern history of psychology. I am sharing a segment about Watson in between the "Foundational" stage and the "Hard Wiring" stage, as earlier stated, Watson was so bold to make the following statement:

"Give me a dozen healthy infants, well formed in my own specified world to bring them up in, and I'll guarantee to take anyone at random and train him to become any type of specialist I might select. Doctor, lawyer, artist, merchant, and yes, even beggar man and thief regardless of his talents, pensions, tendencies, abilities, vocations and race of his ancestors."[6]

John B. Watson

Essentially Watson said that though conditioning and what can be termed behavior reinforcement, he could create the behaviors to make your son or daughter whatever you desired. Watson would write articles in newspapers and magazines and his work led to the now famous Dr. Spock books on raising children.

This message of behaviorism or what many termed "Watsonian Behavior" in the 1920's was extremely popular, as it gave people hope that if you created a proper environment, your children could and would grow up to be anything they wanted to become.

He was routinely declared to be the father of American behaviorism. Watson was interested in Pavlov's work, the Russian physiologist who developed what is known as classical conditioning, yet Watson took it to the next level. Pavlov gave Watson the understanding of how associations are formed and how behavior is shaped.

Watson earned his PhD at the University of Chicago and found his way to Johns Hopkins University in Baltimore, where he studied infants, their behavior and conducts the famous and controversial **Little Albert Experiment** at the famous baby clinic.

Watson was interested in taking Pavlov's research further to show that emotional reactions could be classically conditioned in people.

Little Albert

The participant in the "Little Albert" experiment was a child whom Watson and Rayner called "Albert B.," but is known popularly today as Little Albert. Around the age of nine months, Watson and Rayner exposed the child (Little Albert) to a series of stimuli including a white rat, a rabbit, a monkey, a dog, masks and burning newspapers and observed the boy's reactions. The boy initially showed no fear of any of the objects he was shown.

The next time Albert was exposed to the rat, Watson made a loud noise by hitting a metal pipe located behind the boy with a hammer. Naturally, the child began to cry after hearing the loud noise. After repeatedly pairing the white rat with the loud noise, Albert began to cry simply after seeing the rat.

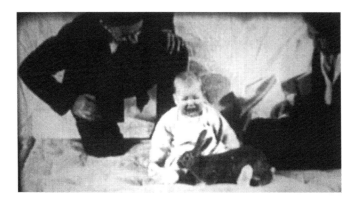

John B. Watson and Rosalie Rayner with "Little Albert"

Watson and Rayner wrote:

"The instant the rat was shown, the baby began to cry. Almost instantly he turned sharply to the left, fell over on [his] left side, raised himself on all fours and began to crawl away so rapidly that he was caught with difficulty before reaching the edge of the table."[7]

The association to the rat was "generalized" to all the animals and shapes. Because of the association to the loud noise and the white rat, when the child sees the white dog, the white rabbit, or even a white Santa Claus face, the baby began to cry and skirmish away.

Unfortunately for Watson, he was essentially forced out of the psychology community as a result of a very public extra-marital affair with his assistant Rosalie Rayner. Watson's wife was a daughter of a well-connected public figure in Baltimore, and she published Watson's love letters to Rayner in the newspaper, which led to his departure from John's Hopkins. Watson went on to become an advertising executive on Madison Avenue where he changed human behavior through advertising. He created the term "keeping up with the Joneses" and was the first to use psychology and the emotion of fear in product advertising.

9

THE HARD WIRING STAGE

Hard Wiring Stage

Hard Wiring Stage (11-18 yrs)

The Hard Wiring Stage is the period of development where <u>7 Principles of Success</u> and <u>Two Guiding Beliefs</u> are "hard-wired" into the human psyche either elevating or limiting ones success in life.

The 7 Principles of Success are as follows:

- Rules – Structure
- Consequences
- Work-Reward Relationship
- Quality of Work
- Drive for More / Drive to Sustain
- Overcoming Obstacles / Perseverance
- Recovery Time

Two Guiding Beliefs

1. Who am I? (Self-image)
2. What's necessary to succeed?

Age 11 – 18 is the Hard Wiring stage, which is considered the most important stage in developing the "wiring for success." During the Hard Wiring stage, children are taught how to succeed in the world by their primary caregivers in addition to their own experience with their environment.

I've shared with you the writings and words of John B. Watson, and how he called out to the American people in an attempt to provide them with the tools to raise their children to be "whatever" they desired. Watson was extremely vocal on this front in the mid 1920's.

Interestingly enough, Aristotle the iconic Greek philosopher who died in 322 B.C. made the statements:

"If parents don't occupy the office of a parent, then they bring into the world a potential deplorable character of a human being."[8]

I believe Aristotle was a bit harsh with the "potential deplorable character" statement, yet what's fascinating to me is the fact the subject of raising successful children has been a point of study and discussion in 322 B.C.

Of the three phases of development in the psycho-success developmental theory (Pre-development stage, Foundational stage and the Hard Wiring Stage), the Hard Wiring Stage is where the "success" wiring takes place. What's right and what's wrong is subjective, and the degrees of structure vary from environment to environment, yet the processes and fundaments of success are incontestable.

Environment - the physical world a child is raised in, including the stimulus, which is the input from parents or primary caregivers, shapes the behavior of the developing human being. John B. Watson proved it in the 1920's and B.F. Skinner reinforced the findings and raised the bar in the 60's and 70's.

How do you define the "stimulus" children receive from parents and primary caregivers as they develop? The best answer - **It's the response to their behavior**.

The responses to the behavior develop the 7 Principles of Success, and those 7 Principles of Success either expand or restrict the developing human's ability to achieve.

10

THE 7 PRINCIPLES OF SUCCESS

Of the Hard Wiring Stage

The 7 Principles of Success

1. Rules – Structure
2. Consequences
3. Work-Reward Relationship
4. Quality of Work
5. Drive for More / Drive to Sustain
6. Overcoming Obstacles / Perseverance
7. Recovery Time

Explanation of 7 Principles for Success

1. <u>Rules</u> – Structure: Children must have Rules and Structure to create the understanding of "how to succeed" in life. As an entrepreneur, I am one to push, bend and break the rules, yet I know the rules in various situations, and I understand their relationship to where I want to go.

Unfortunately for many people, rules have a negative connotation rather than a <u>necessary</u> connotation. In my 7 Principles for Success, I've combined Rules and Structure, as my experience tells me, one leads to the other.

No matter who you are, how old or young, how rich or poor, we live and play by rules. Whether you just turned 16 and you buy your first car, or you are 35 years-old and starting a new company, there are rules that you must abide by in order to drive the car or start the business.

When raising children, it would only make logical sense to prepare the child or young adult to understand "how" to navigate his/her way through life by providing them with rules during the foundational stage and without a doubt, during the Hard Wiring stage. Those parents who fail to provide an environment with rules and structure, are literally misleading their children about what they need to succeed. Whether advancing to college or starting the journey in work world, a lack of understanding and respect for rules leads to underperformance.

2. Consequences: All successful people know there are consequences for every action. A well-developed, responsible adult understands the reality of consequences. Thus any decision made will be followed by consequences.

The principle of consequences has shown to be one of the keys to success. Unfortunately many children are "misled" by their primary caregivers and their environment by not having consequences for breaking agreed upon rules or not following through on agreed upon tasks. These developing adults experience a more difficult time creating traction for success.

Rules, as stated above (Principle #1) precede consequences. For instance, if a child breaks a "rule" and the consequence is real, no matter how mild or severe the consequence is; the child learns the relationship between rules and consequences.

Ben, a 17 year-old junior in high school is in the school band. The school band has assembled a field trip to Ohio State to participate and learn skills to increase their skills and performance. Each student is responsible for $500 fee to participate. The students have four months to plan for the event. With their planned fundraisers, each student will be responsible for $350 on their own to make the trip. Ben really wants to go, so he approaches his parents with the opportunity. Ben's parents want to help Ben so they set up a "participation plan" along with some rules for Ben to earn his way to attend the Ohio State field trip. Ben was tasked with doing his normal chores, along with helping his dad with a weekend project. In addition, Ben was required to have perfect attendance at school, barring sickness of course, as Ben had a pattern of skipping afternoon classes on occasion. Ben and his parents agreed to the plan along with the rules.

Three weeks prior to the field trip, the school had contacted Ben's parents as Ben had skipped two classes on two separate days last week.

A rule had been broken and Ben's parents have choices on how they will handle the situation. My intent is not to give you an opinion about what's right and what's wrong; I'm simply sharing what the research indicates.

In this situation, Ben's parents followed-through with the agreed upon consequences and Ben did not participate in the trip. Although it was a tremendous disappointment to Ben and his parents, Ben experienced a "real-life" consequence for not following the rules. The consequence of "not going on the trip" helped Ben throughout his life, as he remembered the pain and disappointment he felt from not being able to be with his friends on the trip. Ben made the decision to skip class, and thus he experienced the real consequences of not attending his high school band field trip.

Some of the parents I interviewed thought the "punishment" was mean, severe and unnecessary. **The fact is, not going on the field trip wasn't a punishment; it was a consequence**. You can see the similarities to this parental behavior and the situation with the baby crying in the Pre-Development stage of

Psycho-Success Developmental Theory - The loving coddling parents and the loving teaching parent.

The story of Ben and his field trip is just one story, yet there are many potential situations that children and their primary caregivers are encountered with every week.

When the child experiences an environment with no consequences, they are being "fooled" in regards to how things work in the real world. It would be similar to handing a person a map to get to New York, yet the map actually took them to Miami.

Having no consequences during the hard wiring stage is the equivalent of providing the young adult with a road map to mediocrity.

Without real consequences, the decision making process in the young adult is immature and undeveloped and will continue to be a source for setbacks and he or she moves through life.

In order to create what I refer to as "Success Wiring," consequence consistency is imperative.

Consequence consistency relates to how consistent the caregiver is with giving and adhering to consequences for inappropriate behavior or substandard effort or quality of work. A child who experiences consequence consistency understands the relationship to not completing a task to lack of desired results.

For example, the child who was required to perform a series of house or yard chores for an inappropriate action, yet isn't required to complete the chores will not develop the success wiring necessary for success. Pushing through obstacles, experiencing a sense of "completion" is one of the most important "Success Skills" available to a person, and like most of the success wiring, it is a <u>learned skill</u>.

Parents or primary caregivers who do not let their kids experience the pain and disappointment of failure, or don't follow through with their consequences are actually not fostering growth and development. They are essentially robbing the child of his or her success tools, which directly impacts the self-esteem and self-image of the child in a negative manner.

Or when the primary caregiver provides material items with virtually no contribution from the child, the child's "wiring" of what it takes to acquire or create rewards, is underdeveloped and immature.

3. Work – Reward Relationship

The success principle of "work – reward" is an essential part of the success wiring. Jim Rohn referred to this principle as the "law of sowing and reaping."

https://www.youtube.com/watch?v=NY2SWNGJckI

The law of sowing and reaping originated in the Bible.

The law of sowing and reaping reflects the efforts of the farmer. The farmer who plants the corn, along with watering, fertilizing and working the field, will reap/harvest a profitable crop which will both feed his family and provide income. The farmer, who plants the crops yet doesn't "work" the field, will not reap the rewards of the profitable crop. Jim Rohn talks about the farmer who plants the seeds, yet some of which are eaten by the birds. You must keep planting.

I have translated the law of sowing and reaping into the "work – reward" relationship. The work – reward relationship is a learned skill. It's conditioned into the child and young adult from the primary caregiver and the environment.

Children who have no reference to working in order to attain a reward are at a severe disadvantage when participating in the competitive adult world. It's troubling as the young adult who wasn't taught, or wasn't wired for the work – reward relationship actually doesn't "get it" when success doesn't simply appear when they "show up."

Many children go through their entire young lives merely having to "show up" and they are blessed with rewards and gifts. Unfortunately they are being misled about what it takes to succeed by the people who love them the most.

The "work – reward" relationship is an experiential lesson. A person cannot be told about the work-reward relationship, they have to experience it. As humans, we learn by doing. Actually, all organisms learn by doing.

Where's the cheese?

Edward Tollman (April 14, 1886 – November 19, 1959) was an American psychologist. He was most famous for his studies on behavioral psychology specifically using rats in mazes to research cognitive behavior.

Edward Tollman

His major theoretical contributions came in his 1932 book, *Purposive Behavior in Animals and Men*, and in a series of papers in the Psychological Review, "The determinants of behavior at a choice point" (1938), "Cognitive maps in rats and men" (1948) and "Principles of performance" (1955).[9]

Ronnie and Bill

Ever since Ronnie the rat was a young rat, he was placed in the middle of big, confusing maze when it was feeding time. As soon as Ronnie found himself in this unfamiliar place, a nugget of cheese was placed right next Ronnie and he ate. Ronnie the rat learned both cognitively and experientially that the cheese always shows up whenever the feeling of hunger occurs. He doesn't know why, nor does he question it. It just is.

This pattern was duplicated all through Ronnie's young rat life and on into his young adult life.

Conversely, when it was feeding time for Ronnie's friend Rat Bill, Rat Bill was placed on one end of the maze, and the cheese was placed on the opposite end of the maze. Rat Bill worked hard to find the cheese, taking wrong turns and finding empty spaces. As rat Bill matured, he cognitively and experientially learned the effort required to figure out the pattern of the maze in order to find the cheese and satisfy his hunger.

When Ronnie the rat was a young adult, suddenly the game changed. Just as before, Ronnie was placed in the middle of the maze, yet the cheese wasn't dropped right next to him. The cheese was placed at the edge of the maze, to a place Ronnie had never been. Ronnie didn't even know where to start or what to do. Ronnie the rat sat in the middle of the maze, taking a few steps one way, then back, then a few steps the other way, then back... looking for the cheese that had always been there. But the cheese wasn't there. Who would play this cruel joke on Ronnie?

Ronnie's self esteem was impacted in a negative manner, as he couldn't find the cheese. He felt the world was against him. He didn't feel good about himself. Where is the cheese? Don't they know who he is? He's Ronnie the Rat. This pattern continued and Ronnie became weak, both psychologically and physically. His confidence and self-esteem hit an all-time low. He did find the liquor store and started drinking to ease his pain and he spiraled into mediocrity.

How could Ronnie, who was such a promising young rat, become so mediocre and unmotivated?

As with many young humans, during the Foundational stage and the Hardwiring stage of Psycho-Success Development, Ronnie the Rat was robbed of his chance to connect the wiring that would serve him in his adult life. From an outside perspective, it would be unfair to judge

Ronnie for his behavior. He simply did what he was trained and prepared to do. <u>He didn't know that he didn't know.</u>

For instance, the child in the Hard Wiring stage who is given a car, computer, iPads and money with no "work –reward" system in place, has a false understanding of how the world operates. Unfortunately, unbeknownst to the child or young adult, they have skipped a step in the "success wiring," (The work–reward step) and as a result, will feel frustration as they mature and grow into the next stage of their life. "Why aren't things working out for me?"

When a young person has no reference to a work-reward equation, the thought of commitment and completion of a task or job has no sense of reality. This lack of understanding often times stays with the young adult through their entire lives. The young adult can thank the caregiver for that gift.

In all my work and research, my findings indicate parents/caregivers want to do the right thing, yet ironically by not allowing the child to exchange effort for reward, or "go without" or experience disappointment, they are actually preparing the child for mediocrity. If a person has never experienced what it is like to work, persevere and overcome obstacles prior to the adult stage, they are at a severe disadvantage once existing in the real world.

4. **Quality of Work**

John B. grew up in mid-Michigan. It was a beautiful part of the country. Michigan experiences the four seasons: a beautiful spring, a short summer, a glorious fall and a long, cruel winter.

As John B. grew older and strong enough to take-over his fathers duties to shovel the snow, he was excited. His dad had an allowance system in place where John B. would earn money based on his performing jobs and chores around the house. Each and every winter John B. had helped his father shovel snow and was expected to participate more with every year of maturity.

It was late November and then came the first winter snow. John B's dad took him out and showed him how to do the job effectively and how he wanted it done. John B. worked hard for three hours, clearing the walkway from the entry door to the garage, and the area outside the garage to the street.

It was a substantial job for a 13 year-old. John B. was proud of himself. He went inside to get his father to show him his accomplishment. His dad was proud of his hard work and acknowledged

John B for his efforts, yet his dad wasn't satisfied with the overall job.

His dad had an expectation for how the edges of the walkway and driveway area should look. Each edge had to be a straight and vertical edge from the walkway up to the top of the snow line. For instance, if the shoveled snow was 18-inches high from the sidewalk, the edge from each side of the sidewalk was to be straight up and vertical. His dad required a manicured type of finish.

Again, John B's dad was pleased with his effort yet the "quality of work" did not meet his expectations, so his dad required him to "fix" all the edges. All of the edges meant ALL of the edges. The edges from the entryway to the garage had to be fixed, and the edges from the garage driveway to the street and to be fixed.

John B. voiced his frustration with his dad, as he had worked hard on the job. His dad calmly but firmly replied, "a half-ass job will get you a half-ass paycheck. Unfortunately, you don't have a choice to get half your allowance for this job. It's either all or none. Your choice."

John B. went back to work and straightened all the edges to the job's expectations and he received his full earnings. Fortunately for John B, his father required him to perform a high quality of work on everything he did around the house, whether is be mowing the yard, shoveling snow, or washing the cars.

As John B. matured through the hard-wiring phase, he learned what "Quality of work" meant. As a result as he developed into a young, independent man, he was able to advance his career through his adult-life as he understood people who performed a low quality of work, didn't receive the opportunities or advancements of those who had the "Quality of Work" wiring for success.

Children who progress through the foundational and hard-wiring stages without developing the "Quality of Work" wiring typically experience a more difficult time understanding what it takes to be successful in the world. It's not that the children are lazy. The children just weren't wired properly.

They were wired for mediocrity rather than wired for success.

5. <u>Drive for More / Drive to sustain</u>

What gives people that drive to succeed? There are many factors that comprise what gives people drive, yet the drive for more and the drive to sustain is a real factor in the development of success. 84% of people I've interviewed over the course of my career have the drive for more. As a matter of fact, of the 308 people I worked with, 264 possessed the drive for more.

<u>Gina</u>

Gina grows up with a single mother. Her house is filled with love, yet they struggle financially. Gina wears clothes they buy at the Salvation Army store. On very special occasions, her mom buys her a new pair of jeans and a couple of new blouses for school. Gina is on an assisted lunch program at school and she walks both to and from school everyday. Her mom is up early and home late working as a maintenance supervisor for a retail store in their area.

Gina learns how to make herself food as she comes home from school everyday and spends the first few hours on her own prior to her mom coming home. Her after school diet consists of cold sandwiches, soup and tuna. Gina's mom works hard and does the best she's able to, yet they live in a small apartment in Phoenix, AZ. The neighborhood is working class and surrounded by crime. The conversations at the kitchen table are consistently about what they can't have and do. Gina's mom often times talks about how Gina can create a better life for herself by getting good grades and going to college.

Ted

Ted is a young boy who lives in a small, rural town consisting of 2,000 people, most of which are farmers. Ted's father is a school teacher and by the standards of the town that they live in, Ted's father makes a good living. It's a great environment for a young boy to grow up in. Ted has the opportunity to experience activities most city kids don't have the opportunity to do, such as hunting, fishing and camping. On the other hand, the opportunities for anyone growing up in a small town are very limited. It was common for young men and women to graduate from high school and then go to work on the farm and continue the cycle. Other kids went to college to find out what the world has to offer.

Ted was a good kid. He was smart, charismatic and he was good with people. He appreciated the environment he grew up in, yet he knew there was more, and he was committed to finding it. Ted went to college, became and entrepreneur and traveled the world. He was driven to create a different life than he had seen and experienced as a young boy. There was nothing wrong with the small town life, yet he wanted more.

The Drive for more is simple; a child grows up in an environment where he or she is limited by economical or even geographical factors, which prevents them from having material possessions or participating in certain activities. Children who grow up "not having" material possessions and opportunities other children have, or living in an environment less than desirable, develop the drive for more. In simple terms, they want to create a better life for themselves than they were given as a child and young adult. They don't fault their parents or primary care givers for not having, yet they see what others have and a natural human tendency is to want more.

As a result, these children who grow up "not having" have been instilled with the "drive for more." We've all seen stories about people on television who have reached incredible success and they talk about wanting to create a better life for themselves and their family. The drive for more is "success-wiring."

Andrew Carnegie – The Drive for More

Carnegie led the expansion of the steel industry in the late 19th century. In 1848 when Carnegie was 13 years old, his parents emigrated from Scotland with nothing but the clothes on their back and a solid work ethic.

Carnegie's first job in the United States at age 13 was in a Pittsburg cotton mill where he was a "bobbin boy." He changed spools of thread in the cotton mill for 12 hours a day, 6 days a week. His starting wage was $1.20 per week.

In 1850, a short two years later, Carnegie was hired by the Ohio Telegraph Company as a telegraph messenger boy. The messenger boys of the 1850's were similar to New York City bicycle couriers of the present day weaving through the dangerous streets. Carnegie was paid for each mile traveled, so time was of the essence. The messenger boys would pick up hand written and printed messages to be delivered to the Telegraph Company in order to send electronically to its destination. He made

$2.50 per week. Carnegie developed a talent for distinguishing the differing sounds the incoming telegraph signals produced by ear and earned a promotion within a year.

Like other self-made success stories, Carnegie was hungry for both economic success and knowledge. Colonel James Anderson saw the hunger in Carnegie and opened up his personal library of over 400 books for Carnegie to borrow. Carnegie was a consistent "borrower" and improved his knowledge, language and communication skills.

Carnegie was a hustler and by the 1860's he had investments in bridges, oil derricks, railroads and railroad sleeping cars. He built Pittsburgh's Carnegie Steel Company and sold it to J.P. Morgan in 1901 for $480 million, which is the equivalent of approximately $14 billion in 2014.

Carnegie, being one of the wealthiest men in the word in the early 1900's, was a man who wanted to always make personal strides for success as well as give others opportunities to shine.

Carnegie believed that the process of success could be outlined in a simple formula that anyone would be able to understand and achieve. He then commissioned Napoleon Hill to interview and analyze 500 of the most successful men and women in order to discover and publish the formula for success.[10]

The Drive to Sustain

The drive to sustain is a result of a child growing up in an affluent environment, yet held to standards, accountability and taught the work – reward relationship. Donald Trump's children would be a solid example. There are countless wealthy Americans who raise mediocre children, yet Donald Trump understands what it takes to be successful, and he made certain his children possessed those attributes.

In my years of advising high-level professionals, I can't tell you how many times I've heard the phrase "I just don't want to screw up my kids." Think about it... high level executives, entertaining guests, conducting business meetings and consistent travel demands. How is it possible to be present with the children they are raising? There are methods to ensure the connection, yet it's a challenge for many people. Human behavior indicates the need to overcome the guilt of not being present by making sure the children have everything they need, and that typically translates into skipping the step of the work-reward relationship. As a result, we have countless children of affluent families who have no clue on how to create results in their own lives.

Donald Trump's children had the potential to fit the profile of the "wealthy mediocre," yet he instilled in his children the same wiring that allowed him to succeed. Donald held his kids to certain standards. All of his children had responsibilities and consequences for their actions.

Ivanka Trump is Donald's second child and first daughter born October 30, 1981. She is the executive vice president of Development and Acquisitions at The Trump Organization. She is also the principle of Ivanka Trump Fine Jewelry and the Ivanka Trump Lifestyle Collection, which includes fragrance, handbags, footwear, outerwear and eyewear collections.

She graduated summa cum laude in 2004 from the Wharton School of Business at the University of Pennsylvania. She is the author of The Trump Card: Playing to Win in Work and in Life.

The drive to sustain is simply the fortune of growing up with a "comfortable" life, yet having the drive to sustain the lifestyle one has been accustomed to. On the other hand, one that has been shown a life of "comfort" and has not been "wired for success," often proves to be an underachiever blaming the world for not understanding them. From the outside looking in, it would be difficult for a person to feel sorry for the underachiever from a childhood of wealth, but the reality is the "underachiever" is unaware of "how" to create success in their lives.

Case in Point: Ronnie the Rat

6. <u>Overcoming Obstacles / Perseverance</u>

The ability to overcome obstacles is paramount for success. No success story has occurred without perseverance. As my good friend Rudy says, "It's always too soon to quit."

I challenge you to find a success story that lacks overcoming obstacles or perseverance as an ingredient. Bill Gates, Oprah Winfrey, Abraham Lincoln, Martin Luther King or Andrew Carnegie; anyone who has accomplished anything significant possessed the ability to overcome obstacles.

Overcoming obstacles and perseverance is a gift that is given from the caregiver to the child during the foundational stage and the Hard Wiring Stage. Providing the Work-Reward relationship along with "quality of work" instills the drive for more. Without the drive for more, there is no perseverance; there is no working though the tough times.

When one is consistently shown the easy way out, or thrown a rescue device at the first sign of struggle or defeat, the "hard-wiring" is not connected. Again, to say the person who doesn't possess perseverance was lazy or a quitter would be a harsh judgment, as disappointingly they were never taught, shown or programmed how to do that.

7. Recovery Time

Recovery Time is a term I created that applies to how fast a person is willing to overcome their challenges and get back on the track to success. Successful people make the choice to make their recovery time shorter, rather than longer.

Have you ever met someone who was faced with a challenge or setback and they allowed it to turn into a bad month, a bad 6-months or even a bad year? Sounds crazy doesn't it... yet I bet most of you know someone who has made the choice to turn a setback into a long slump.

Recovery time is the result of The Drive for More/The Drive to sustain, along with one important factor – No Back Door. I'm using No Back Door as a term for not having someone available to come to your rescue as soon and you spill some milk.

During the Hard-Wiring stage, the success principle of Recovery Time is developed when the young adult has to "brush themselves off" after a disappointment and "get back on their horse."

11

TWO GUIDING BELIEFS

Of The Hard Wiring Phase

Two Guiding Beliefs

From the Hard Wiring stage of the psycho-success developmental theory, two powerful and impactful beliefs are formed in the child:

1. <u>A belief about "who I am." – Self-Image, Self-Esteem and Identity</u>

Because of the child's experiences in the physical world, they develop beliefs that can empower or dis-empower the child throughout life.

A child raised in an environment with consequences, rules and respect, along with love and guidance are prone to develop beliefs that will empower the child throughout the Hard Wiring stage and beyond.

Beliefs such as:

- I'm a hard worker
- I perform quality work
- I can do anything
- I'm a good kid
- People like me
- People want to help me succeed
- I am a winner
- I am successful

- When I complete a task with quality work, I get a reward. (Money, praise, opportunities)
- No matter what happens, I can get it done.

On the other hand, a child that is raised in an environment with no rules, no consequences, lack of respect and a lack of guidance are prone to develop beliefs that will limit the child throughout the Hard Wiring stage and beyond.

Examples could be one or more of the following:

- I always screw things up
- I'm lazy
- There are no opportunities "out there" for someone like me.
- People are always making it hard for me.
- People don't like me.
- I'm a loser

2. **The Belief about "what it takes" to be successful in the world**.

Again, based on their experiences and observations in the hard wiring stage, children develop beliefs about "What it takes to be successful in the world."

Empowering beliefs could be one or more of the following:

- If I want something, I can attain it through hard work
- Things don't just magically appear, I have to put in work and effort
- Working hard and performing quality work will earn me rewards (praise or monetary)
- Doesn't matter what I choose to do, I'll get what I want
- Good quality work, along with consistency will bring me the rewards I desire.

Disempowering beliefs:

- You need to be lucky or have a rich family to be successful
- It's all about whom you know.
- Doesn't matter what I do, people don't like me.
- My parents always bail me out, so it doesn't matter what I do.
- If I cry or complain long enough, I get what I want.
- Excuses bail me out of anything.
- The system holds me down.

12

FAULTY WIRING

Faulty Wiring

Faulty wiring is a term I use for those who grew up in a privileged environment and reaped the material rewards of life without learning the 7 Principles of Success.

They haven't learned the 7 Principles of Success, yet they enjoy all the fruits of their predecessors labor. As a result they have developed faulty wiring. Actually, no wiring would be a more accurate statement – they have an expectation they will be provided with material things and opportunities just because they always have.

Many people live their entire lives "getting" yet have never learned the 7 principles. Unfortunately for those who lose their cash flow, their trust fund, their parents or their fortune, they have no understanding of how to create it on their own. These people were provided "faulty wiring" as a developing child and a young adult.

Success

Being in the success industry for 20 years and studying human behavior for 30 years, I've encountered multiple reasons and myths on why people become successful and achieve success in our culture.

First of all, lets define success in relationship to our conversation in this specific book.

I am defining success as:

"A person's individual or group achievements based on his or her actions. A desired outcome that was achieved as a result of a consistent pattern of behavior."

That's what it's really about… creating success in your life on a blank canvas, or creating success in your life with the cards you've been dealt.

<u>Born into it</u> – Yes, without a doubt, many people who have acquired wealth, or should I say, live as if they have acquired wealth, were fortunate to be born into wealth… or maybe it's unfortunate. Depends on the psychological skill level of the individual. There are examples of notable people in our culture that were presented with opportunities that others just didn't have. Yet being born into opportunity does not ensure a feeling of success or happiness.

People who were children of successful people have the opportunities and the financial resources for achievement, yet often times have not developed the necessary psychology to build a foundation for success, not to mention a model of the world others can relate with.

Canadian wealth advisor Franco Lombardo studied the effects of wealthy in relationship to their kids and how their kids were psychologically prepared for the real world. In his book, "The Great White Elephant, Why Rich Kids Hate their Parents," Lombardo indicates that within wealthy families, the emotional components to create a "successful" adult are not being dealt with.[11]

Lombardo sites three common reasons:

1. Wealthy parents just don't say "no" enough, thus the child grows up with a sense of getting whatever they want. They go out into the real world and the world tells them "no," they get angry and have resentment for their parents.

Ironically true from my perspective, as I've coached and counseled many of these wealthy parents. The same parents that have the knowledge of what it takes to be successful and often times cheat their kids and set them up for failure with their lack of functional ability to create results in the world.

2. Time. Wealthy parents are often time absent parents, which is why the children get cheated as stated above. Kids feel abandoned. Human

nature is to make up loss of time with money, which doesn't work. The only way to make up for loss of time, is time.

3. Society. Society in large makes fun of rich kids and often times parents tell their kids to hide their wealth at an early age, and when kids grow up, they feel like much of their identity has to be hidden.

In summary, there are many young men and women who drive nice cars, go out for fine dinners and live in nice houses. They have access to money, yet they are not wired for success. They don't have the emotional or psychological skills to overcome obstacles, persevere, grind it out and do what it takes to succeed.

According to Lombardo, many children of wealthy families are not **Wired for Success**. One of my clients who I respect deeply said it best:

If a baby lion is given food past the age of infancy; if the baby lion is given the "keys to the jungle" without having to develop the skills to hunt, defend or attack, the lion is living in a world of make believe; he is underdeveloped in his ability to thrive in the jungle.

If a person is given all the rewards of success with no sense of "earning" or developing their skills, they don't have the psycho-success development necessary to achieve success. As a matter of fact, they will have no drive or ambition to do so. When the baby lion is given fresh food, shelter, and all the necessities for a comfortable life, they never acquire the inner-wiring of hunger, ambition and drive.

As a human being, drive comes from not having something you want.

There are no shortcuts to having the psychology necessary to achieve success. Without the trials, the setbacks, the failures, the obstacles and the evidence of achievement through consistent action, the human being has no confidence to create or achieve their dreams.

Let me be very clear; developing the "Wiring for Success" is not limited to those who come from poverty-stricken backgrounds. The theory on Psycho-Success development proves the fact that success principles are developed at socioeconomic levels. Below are three examples of notable American success stories; all of which come from different economic backgrounds.

- Steve Jobs – Born February 1955. Both his primary caretakers, (adoptive parents) Paul & Clara Jobs were not college graduates. Paul was a mechanic and a carpenter and Clara was an accountant. Steve had what would be categorized as a median income childhood. He received a partial academic scholarship to Reed College, yet the college was far too expensive for his mom & dad. Steve dropped out of college and through a series of entrepreneurial experiments; he and his business partner Steve Wozniak, formed Apple Computer in his father's garage. Steve didn't have a trust or access to seed money to start Apple, so he and Wozniak had to create the results to survive.   Steve's   psycho-success development served his journey, as he was fired from his own company (Apple), started NeXT Computer in 1985 and through hustle and determination, acquired The Graphics Group (Pixar) and reunited with Apple in 1996.[12]

• <u>Oprah Winfrey</u> – Born January 29th, 1954. Oprah was born in rural Mississippi to an unwed teenage mother who was a housemaid. Shortly after her birth, Oprah lived in rural poverty for six years with her maternal grandmother who was so poor that she wore potato sacks as dresses and was made fun of by the local children.[13] Oprah moved back and forth from mother to grandmother. At 13, after years of suffering, Oprah ran away from home.[14]

When she was 14 years-old, she became pregnant but her son died after birth.[15] Oprah's first job in high school was at the grocery store.[16]

Deemed one of the most successful business people in the world, many are familiar with Oprah's story. Aligning with the psycho-success theory of development, Oprah was wired for success by developing the ability to overcome obstacles and recover from setbacks. She had a belief, a self-image of what she could be and she held on to that image over her developmental stage.

• Donald Trump – June 14, 1946, born to Fred and Mary Anne Trump in Queens, New York. Although Donald had a comfortable childhood, he was sent to NYMA (New York Military Academy) at age 13 where he learned discipline and gained his competitive edge. People have the perception that Donald Trump was a "silver spooner," yet his competitive drive, determination and ability to overcome obstacles is what has made Trump one of the most successful and celebrated businessmen in American history. Donald learned the real estate business by working with his father's company, Elizabeth Trump and Son, which focused on middle-class housing in Brooklyn, Queens and Staten Island. He made his own mark in New York City on hustle, determination and desire.[17]

The financial resources available during a child's upbringing, or lack thereof is not the primary factor of creating the "wiring for success," it's the success tools developed by the child during the three stages of Psycho-Success development.

13

INTERVIEW

Rudy Ruettiger:

RUDY was one of the most impactful and inspirational movies of all time. The movie has crossed generations as the story is about a young man from a working class family who had a dream to attend prestigious Notre Dame.

I had the opportunity to talk with Rudy about his journey and what it takes to be successful:

Dan: Rudy, everyone knows about your story about when you went to Notre Dame, but what was your family life growing up before you went to Notre Dame? Where did you get the skills or what I refer to as "wiring" to make that happen?

Rudy: That's a great question. When you grow up in a large family, you are delegated certain odd jobs or chores for the family. Sometimes on your own, or other times you have to work together as a family. But what really happens are two dynamics. There is a little bit of "you don't have what the other kids have", whom you go to school with.

I would say to myself, "Well, why can't we have that?" Just like your theory on success Dan, you develop a bit of an attitude, a drive. I never understood how hard my father worked when I was a child, because you don't see him working three jobs. You know he's working, but you don't understand the dynamics of that.

I would say to myself, "Wait a minute, why does my friend's dad have things and my dad doesn't have it?" So your attitude grows to an area of "I'm going to go earn and improve my situation as an adult, not an entitlement as you may see quite a bit in today's youth.

I developed an "earn-to attitude" through the process of watching my father work three jobs to take care of his family. I said, to myself, "Oh, okay, I get it now. **The way to get it is to work for it.** That was my development.

The other important development part for me is was not to listen to people who label you, or who put people in a box." Whether it's in education, whether it's in jobs, or whatever, unfortunately people don't take a look at the kid's heart.

People not giving people the benefit of the doubt, just because you grew up on the other side of the tracks, or your father didn't have a prestigious job. That's where I became angry at those types of people: specifically educators and coaches. That's one of the reasons, the big reason why I did the movie, "Rudy", because I was more upset with Notre Dame's mentality.

Notre Dame's attitude was slanted toward the elite. Guys like me couldn't get the edge. Guys like me couldn't get the benefit of the doubt. That's who Notre Dame was; catering toward the elite. That was their culture. Does that make sense?

The only reason I was able to get into Notre Dame is I fought. I wouldn't and didn't take no for an answer. I grew up fighting for everything, not literally, yet I had to fight for every break I got. It was in my body from my upbringing. I had developed the attitude of, "Okay, I'm going to show you that I deserve this too."

I didn't have the academic status these other kids had, but I didn't know I had a learning disorder. All these things you go through as a child that develop your ability to persevere and fight.

It's fascinating how teachers who are teaching these kids, don't seem to understand the earn-it, let's help them attitude. To me, it doesn't matter how fast they learn, as long as they learn it.

That particular mentality is what angered me, because I found out once I went to the Navy, all that stuff is thrown out the window. All the education and the levels of elite and average... were thrown out the window. In the Navy, everyone was the same.

In the Navy you become a team. You've got to work as a team, whether you like that guy or not. You got to live with that guy you don't like. So I learned about teamwork and accomplishing tasks and goals. I said to myself, "Wow, this is a twist." My whole attitude changed in the military. At that point I looked at my childhood life and said to myself, "Well, okay, that's where the chip came from."

I was duped. I was duped by people. I use the word "duped", but maybe someone else would you call it "naïve." I just didn't know what I didn't know.

But when people discover they can do what they dream about, and there are other ways of getting it, they have a whole new attitude.

They don't have to be the sharpest guy in the room.

I had a teacher who said, "You're sure not the brightest light bulb in the classroom." When they say that, that hurts your feelings, and you say to yourself as a young person, "Okay, so I'm stupid," right?

That's what they're saying.

But I found out that the guys who have dreams and goals and who fight for their way were actually the smart ones.

Many of those kids in my class in high school or at Notre Dame didn't have the "fight" that I had. It was all those people who told me I was stupid and couldn't go to Notre Dame, or even achieve success, or that I was to small or too short to play football at Notre Dame... it was all those people who caused me to fight and achieve.

So my success attitude came through. I was not an entitlement attitude, but an "earn-it" attitude, "Why not me?" attitude. The attitude of " I'm going to find a way to get it". That was a change for me that was the result of having to work and scrap as a young boy.

The game-changer for me was boot camp in the Navy. Boot camp really woke me up. The game-changer was learning that everybody's the same. How hard do you want to put your effort across, to learn what you need to know so you can do what you need to do?

Instead of buying into what other people say you are, you can create your own dream through hard work and vision.

FAMILY

I grew up with seven sisters and six brothers and I watched my father work his tail off, and my mother work so hard taking care of all of us. I feel that was the difference. Watching my parents actually work hard and go through the tough times, it showed me what I was supposed to do. That was the difference. Working hard was shown to me from my parents. Working hard was in my DNA.

I watched both my father and my mother die recently, and then you get another level of life understanding and life appreciation. The learning lesson is, you know what? They died happy. They didn't have much, but they died happy.

To me, happiness is the key.

MONEY

Through this journey of business, understanding money was another thing I learned in my life. All the crap I thought I needed that I didn't need. It's just a lesson. We've all heard the cliché' before that money doesn't make you happy, and it's true.

That's one of the reasons I enjoy connecting with you Dan. You are a real guy. You are successful in business and you care about people. You respect people and have solid relationships.

Me personally, I love to inspire people. I know you know the feeling Dan. I get excited when I get around people and feel, "What I see in you is something bigger than you see in you." I love that.

Dan, I respect what you've accomplished because you've been through that same thing I've been through, but in a different way.

Though I don't know about your childhood, but you were in basketball. You played college basketball at a high level. You won two straight national championships. Not a lot of people can say that. Basketball is strategy; basketball is hard work. You're smart; I mean, you have some gifts there, and some talent. But at the same time, I think you didn't feel you were entitled to any of this stuff, so you had to earn your success.

Dan Lier: You're absolutely right. I didn't have parents who were giving me a free ride. I had to figure out a way to make it happen, which as you know, turned out to be a blessing.

Having the skills to figure things out on your own is priceless.

Dan: So Rudy, you went from high school, then to Notre Dame. Then you went to the...

Rudy: No, no. I went from high school to work. I went to work, because I barely got out of high school. It was a fairly challenging time in my life, because of how I felt about myself. I thought I was stupid because teachers labeled me as that.

Like I said, they would say things to my parents. "Your son is a slow learner. He's not coachable or even not teachable.

I had a learning disorder; they didn't understand that. So they classified me as, "the guy is stupid". And as a kid, that's what you bought into.

So after high school I went to work at a power plant. My father worked in an oil refinery. The mentality was, "We're blue collar. This is where we're going to stay. This is what you're going to do for the rest of your life. This is it, buddy."

As I went to work, day after day I thought to myself, "I don't like this. This is not me. I don't want to be like my brother, or my uncles. I want to go do something with my life."

While I was working in the power plant, I had all these same feelings of being unhappy, but I had a good job. It was a union job. People would feel blessed to have a union job, which meant union wages and you had a pension. Many of my friends in the same position felt blessed and they were all set for the next 30 to 35 years. I should say they felt blessed to have a steady job, but none of them really wanted to be there. It's just kind of what you were supposed to do.

We were working our tails off, yet people would tell us we had a great job and we were all set. But working in the power plant you get different jobs, and to make a long story short, I didn't want that experience; that was bottom line. That's when I made the decision to change my destiny. It was during the Vietnam era; I made a decision to change my environment and I chose to go into the Navy.

Ironically after the Navy, I came back to work for the same power plant, and because of my experience in the Navy, I had a better job than before I left. I realized very quickly that I didn't want to be there.

The great thing about it was after my experience in the Navy, I had a different perspective of myself, which was the big key for me. I had a different perspective of me.

I realized it and I knew I didn't want to be there. I had befriended an older guy at work. The older guy, myself and and a younger friend - we were always saying, "We've got to get the heck out of here."

When my one of my friends at the plant made a bad choice and was killed, that's when I said, "Life is too short. I'm out of here. What did I have to lose? I've got nothing to lose and everything to gain. What am I going to lose by trying?"

Dan Lier: That's interesting Rudy, because many guys would say that, yet wouldn't do it; and you did it. That says a lot about you.

Rudy: And I was still young at the time. When I quit the job, my parents never understood that, which led to the conflict with my father. My dad said, "So, what are you going to do? You're leaving a union job?" My dad was a union guy and to him, security and job with the union was what I was supposed to do.

My dad said, "You can't do this." I said, "I am." And that's when I headed to the fantasyland of Notre Dame.

And it was a total fantasy, Dan. I'm not kidding. It was an absolute fantasy journey. It's like going to Hollywood and saying, "I want to make my movie." It just doesn't happen.

I was 23 years old and I showed up at Notre Dame and went to the admissions office and said, "I want to go to Notre Dame." "Okay?" The reality was I didn't have the grades or the money to go to Notre Dame, yet I wanted to make it happen. It was a dream for me.

At 23, I had learned a ton of lessons. I was different from when I graduated from high school at 18. With the Navy experience, then back working at the power plant, and a friend dying – I was different.

Now I had a "want-to" mindset rather than a "why-not" attitude." For me, it was a "want-to" and a "how-to". So I combined the want-to and the how-to attitude and I was focused on how I could go to school at Notre Dame. That mindset led me to find out about the junior college. I couldn't get in to Notre Dame so I had to find a way to get in, and junior college was the door for me.

The junior college really opened my eyes to success. There were only 150 kids in the school, which made it awesome, and we were right across the street from Notre Dame.

Flashback to years ago when I was working at the power plant, I was at a Notre Dame football game with my girlfriend, and I said to her, "I'm going to Notre Dame and I'm committed." She said, "You can't do that. You've got your job and all that stuff." And I said, "No, I'm leaving." That's kind of like how it was shown in the movie; it was shown differently, but that's how it happened.

So now fast-forward to junior college, the admissions counselor told me, "You're going to have a tough time, but you know what, we'll help you in whatever way you want." Just the fact that they said they would help really encouraged me.

From that point, success came from people helping me, and teaching me things I needed to know. Not the things so much in the classroom, yet what I needed to know about being successful.

So I took courses that I should take. I didn't have to take those upper-level courses to go to Notre Dame, and I didn't know that. I just needed to take parallel courses that they would accept, and would satisfy the entry standards. In addition, you didn't have to take SAT or ACT test to go to Notre Dame. That eliminated a lot of pressure right there.

Lastly, they told me my GI Bill would pay for my schooling. That was incredible. So that took care of the economic pressure. Then they offered me an extra job and little things to earn some money while I was there as well. I believed I could do this, and what I found is you get a lot of doors opened when you go towards what you want.

So that taught me another lesson of why people are held back, or why people move forward. As we go through life, we run into people that kill our dreams; I call them "door-stoppers."

These people stop you every time you try to get through the door. "No, you can't come in here." Well, "Guess what, I am coming in, and you need to get out of my way." That was the attitude that I learned, but of course I did it in a nice way.

I also found when you push past the "door-stoppers," often times they became your allies too. I learned that I had to build allies, because you can't do it by yourself, you know? You need people to really help you in little steps.

On the business side, over time I learned that you must be willing to push through door-stoppers. These are lessons you learn when you're in a position that you must earn. Like anything else, you've go to earn your success. It's not easy, but in the long run I'd rather have it that way than having it given to you. As you know Dan, when people are given things without having to earn them, they don't appreciate it, and they don't know how to get it done.

Dan Lier: Yes, without question. That's the primary reason we are having this conversation. I know you, and I know the steps you took to build your success. In my Theory of Psycho-Success, which explains what I call "the wiring" for success, it's proven that people who are given the silver platter, don't know how to get the gold platter, or worse, they don't have the psychology or the fundamentals to keep the silver platter.

Rudy: Right, and here's the biggest lesson I'm learning now. I'm 65, and I'm learning this: There are people in your life who are out there, who don't want to earn it. They just want to attach themselves to you, so they can benefit from who you are. I've learned so much over the past five years. You think a guy is on your team, but he's really not. People come into your life in different disguises.

I've learned a lot about character. To me, character is a big part of being a successful person. Many people are just chasing the dollar. They want to be rich. That's a red flag, right there. I didn't know that. I was naïve. There are people out there who are financially successful, but they're not people you want to be around. I was a slow learner.

For me, I love people who do great things, and big things, and do the right things. I love people who want to be rich, but want to distribute their wealth differently. I don't want to be around people who are wealthy and selfish, and they're more worried about who's going to take their money than how they're going to give their money away. You know the saying; when you die, you can't take it with you.

When you die, it's over. We all know that, yet we're not dead yet, so it's not over. But you know what? It's going to be over some day.

And when it's over:

- What have you done?
- What have you achieved in a way that you leave a legacy behind?

A legacy does a heck of a lot more than how many Superbowls you won. People really don't care. Maybe in the moment they care, but they forget really fast.

So my life of overcoming adversity is definitely related to what you call the "Wiring for Success." My finding a way to go to school at Notre Dame when no one from my family or my neighborhood thought it was possible was because I wanted more. I had a dream and I had no back door. I had no "comfort zone" that many people grow up with.

Me actually getting the "RUDY" movie made was a direct result of hard work and the success wiring. It wasn't about talent. I had no business being in Hollywood making a movie, but I had a dream and I kept going.

I remember a long time ago when our kids went trick or treating together how I was telling you the story of when I was selling cars and telling people about my story at Notre Dame. People would tell me, "wow, you should write a movie." That sounded great, but I didn't know anything about movies.

Getting the movie made is an amazing story in itself.

Dan Lier: You recently wrote a book about that story, right Rudy?

Rudy: Yes. The title is RUDY, my story. It's the story about my journey and how we made the film RUDY.

Dan Lier: Thank you Rudy. It's always a pleasure spending time with you... and continued success.

14

THE WIRING OF RELATIONSHIPS

Relationships

Can you be wired for success or failure in relationships? The answer is YES.

Far too many books have been written about success in life, i.e., how to make more money or grow your business, yet we all know having access to money yet not finding peace, love and balance in your relationship takes much of life's joy away. Not having success in a relationship leaves humans with an empty heart and a longing to be loved and accepted.

As an expert in human behavior, I am quick to point out that I have been unsuccessful in marriage in the past. Does being divorced mean that I, or anyone else is not good at relationships? No is the answer to that question. If not, what does being divorced mean? Actually, it doesn't mean anything except the relationship in the past didn't work.

The concept of attaching meaning to culturally designed failures or successes is a falsehood.

Anyone that is reading this book right now has a belief about what a successful relationship is supposed to be, feel or look like. We get these beliefs from movies, TV shows, friends and most often, from family. Most of our own personal models for relationships come from our family. Specifically what we experienced when we were growing up. Humans learn from observing and doing. One of my mentors, Albert Bandura, who is one of the top behavior psychologists in the world, taught what was called "observational learning." A term that simply means humans learn from the observation of others.

Let's think about that concept for a minute. Let's use a general statement and say that all of us learn about relationships from people we observed the most as we made our journey from a child, to an adolescent, to an adult. With that being said, the many people we observed, modeled or imitated in regards to relationships… they didn't have a clue. Who taught them? Did the people that you and I observed while growing up go to a relationship school, communication school or any type of social psychology training? I'm going to make a general assumption and answer for all of us… No.

So in essence, we base our view on what a successful relationship is or should be on what we saw from people who were never trained or educated on HOW to engage in a successful relationship. With that being said, it makes logical sense why the divorce rate is over 50%?

For me personally, my journey to find the answers were from experience, as I didn't have a mentor to talk about love, emotions or intimacy.

My first wife, who is a great women, we were boyfriend-girlfriend for 7 years. We dated late in college, then long distance in grad school, then a few years while we were attempting figure out life. I felt obligated. I felt like marrying her was what I was supposed to. So I did. I loved her as a person, yet wasn't in love with her. The relationship ended two years after marriage. We both knew engaging in divorce and going our separate ways was the right thing to do. We were young and still had much growing to do, both emotionally and spiritually.

My next unsuccessful journey was a tough one. We dated for approximately six months and she became pregnant. She wanted to have the baby and I couldn't imagine my child growing up with out me having impact as a father, so we went all in. She was fresh out of college at 22 and I was 31.

I was working for Tony Robbins at the time and living in 5 cities a year for 2-3 months each. It was a very unusual life-style, yet we did it. We had our son in 1996 and continued to travel. Our daughter was born in 1998. From 1996 until 2000, we lived in a bubble - an unrealistic, yet safe world of new cities, new experiences and constant change. I lived in 5 cites prior to her coming out "on the road" with me, and together we lived in 25 cities over a five year period. When we settled in California in 2000, with a four-year-old son and two-year-old daughter, we attempted to establish some type of what others would refer to as normalcy. For us, being in one place, with the same stores, the same people and building a life was abnormal. Our journey for learning "outside the bubble" had started in 2000 and it ended in 2006.

The game summary is the relationship didn't make it. It wasn't that we weren't committed to the relationship or took the easy way out. It ended, just like it was supposed to. If you were to ask her what happened, her story is far different from mine, yet that is inherently the challenge for many couples... they don't live in the same world.

Living in the same world is a phrase I'm using to describe someone's model of the world, meaning how things are or are supposed to be. All humans have a different model of the world, depending on culture, experience, social economics and education.

My twenty plus years of research has brought me to what I call the (PWT) "Parallel world theory," which simply means those people whose worlds closely align, have the best chance of creating a loving, lasting and unique bond. The only way to find out if your worlds are aligned is by spending time with one another and being honest and true about your experiences.

People are who they are... and that's who they are. If you meet someone you find fascinating yet they don't live in a world that is parallel to your world, whether logically, emotionally or what it means to love, it's not going to work. The challenge is we are all emotional creatures and the feeling of love and the fear of loss will cause us to make poor decisions if we don't have the education.

Being in the "success" business, I'm consistently facilitating honest, real and vulnerable conversations, whether in a corporate training situation or in an executive coaching relationship. Not long ago one of my clients said, "hey Dan, can I ask you something?" I said of course, and he continued, "you are a positive, successful guy; why did you get a divorce? My response: I married the wrong person. He simply shook his head "yes" as his mind had quickly left the present and was deep in thought.

The fact is that my ex-wife was not the right person for me, yet she is the right person for someone else. She is right someone who lives in her world. And just to be clear, there is no right and wrong world. What gives "my world" the designation of the "right world?" What gives me, or you for that matter, to judge someone based on how they think and operate in the world. Judging someone for how you think they should be, act or respond, is a pompous and arrogant stance. If we use the PWT (Parallel World Theory) and understand the outcome is to find someone whose world is parallel to ours.

In relationships there is no right and wrong, there's just unhappy or happy. When you can find that person whose world is parallel to yours, some may call it "living on the same planet," then you have a chance to find total love, acceptance and inner peace. You have no chance when you are living with an alien.

When I met my wife Jennifer in late 2008, I had been single for two years and had continued my learning and growth process with a goal to discover relationship happiness. I met her on a Southwest airlines flight, and I told her what I had told every other woman I had met after my divorce; I'm never getting married again. It sounds like a good line or set up, yet I was serious about that statement and it did set a good tone for me when I met women for the first time. We dated for a year and it was obvious to me that Jennifer was from the same world that I was from and she solidified my Parallel World Theory.

When we met, Jennifer was 37 and I was 45. She had traveled the world many times over as a headline singer, performer, back-up singer and impersonator. She had been on an international reality show (The Entertainer with Wayne Newton) and finished second. She had traveled on private jets with some of the legends in entertainment such as the Eagles and Christina Aguilera. She was currently headlining a show in Vegas. She had accomplished more and experienced more of life at 37 than most.

As we spent more time together and grew closer, our similar experiences paved the way for mutual respect, understanding and appreciation for what we each did for a living and had accomplished in our lives. Even though from different industries, there was a mutual respect in regards to what it took to prepare and deliver a solid performance no matter what the situation.

I had won two straight national basketball championships as a young man, was accustomed to signing autographs in college and high school, which is not the norm for most. I had been on national TV with consistency, been on some of the biggest stages as a "corporate motivational speaker" and had a best selling book. We both were accustomed to achieving a certain level of success and we both appreciated it and understood that none of that would be possible without having connection with other people, whether that be agents, fans, business associates, good friends and family. We lived in parallel worlds and this was an experience that was a first for both of us.

Parallel World Theory (PWT)

The PWT will create a connection between people and the ability to communicate in a manner that just won't happen otherwise. For Jennifer and me, the PWT was our experiences through her entertainment and my business. Neither one of us is looking for fame or to be recognized for some Hollywood accomplishment.

We both had accomplished a sense of recognition on a smaller scale, and knew that fame itself is not the answer to happiness and a feeling of love and acceptance. Don't get me wrong, we both strive for accomplishment, yet if we could both do what we do in Idaho and stay under the radar, we would. We enjoy our time together, dinners and time with the kids.

When I'm coaching men & women on PWT in regards to relationships, I'm very clear when I say people can have parallel worlds because of their background. If one person is a lawyer and the other is a schoolteacher, they still can have parallel worlds.

People that grew up in the Midwest have certain values that all Midwesterners appreciate. Many factors can influence the PWT. If your father was a banker and you are dating a banker, you can appreciate and respect what your partner's lifestyle and demands are, thus creating a parallel world.

The PWT is why we continue to see people in Hollywood tie the knot, even though life-long relationship success in "tinsel town" is predictably disappointing. Actors and entertainers can relate to one another. Their models of the world are parallel, which leads to a closeness and a feeling of trust.

Currently Tiger woods has been dating downhill skiing champion Lindsay Vonn. Ultimately no one knows what will become of this relationship, yet the PWT is the basis of the relationship. They both respect each other's accomplishments, what it takes to achieve, and the demands of the media, sponsors and physical training. At the end of the day, like anyone else, only their ability to communicate honestly and make adjustments will determine whether they will make it or not.

15

REDEFINING SUCCESS IN RELATIONSHIPS

Redefining Success in Relationships

In my journey for happiness and fulfillment in my relationship has brought me to the conclusion that developing as a person in order to attract the right partner takes learning. A learning that can only come from experience and self-discovery and relationship maturity.

In the United States of America, our cultural rules indicate that we are supposed to get married and stay with our spouse through good times and bad times. The words were written with the best of intent. Those words are considered cultural rules, and a person not staying true to those cultural rules is considered to be a failure. As I stated earlier in the chapter, judging someone else by your rules in pompous, arrogant and quite frankly, ignorant.

Failure is continuing to stay in an unhappy relationship because other people, whether your parents, friends or society thinks you should stay in it. Those who may judge you don't know how you feel on the inside. Unfortunately people will judge you. You just need to understand that people judging you is going to happen either way. People will judge you if you stay in the relationship or you end the relationship. You must make the choice for you.

When I decided to move toward a divorce, I didn't care what others thought, as they weren't feeling or experiencing what I was feeling. Whether I was unhappily married or divorced, I was committed to being a great father, and that's what I did. No doubt there were some bumps along the way, and there still are, yet feeling peace and the ability to communicate with your partner is priceless. I would make that choice again tomorrow.

The message here is only a small percentage of people find the right partner on the "first take." Because most of us have never been taught about what it takes to maintain a successful relationship, there is learning along the way. A learning that only comes from being in a relationship. Some people have been married for 40 years, and unhappy for 40 years... I don't consider that a success. Again, success in a relationship is finding that person who sees you for who you are and accepts you for you. If it takes someone a few times to find that person, than so be it.

Relationship Rules:

There are no good or bad relationships – Relationships are tricky; they are emotional, passionate, exciting, disappointing and come with no blueprint for success. Think about it, in most other goals we attempt to accomplish, whether physical fitness, financial success or learning a new language, we have the equivalent of a blueprint or instruction manual available to assist us find success.

Not so with relationships. Yes, you can buy a plethora of books in the field of relationships, yet there is no blueprint because no one knows your specific emotional make-up, your model of the world and how those two parameters will mold with the person you may be dating.

The point being is that all your previous relationships have taught you about yourself and about what type of partner you need to fulfill your heart. Your previous relationships have taught you about relating with others. That's what a relationship is… relating with another person. For me personally, I am so thankful for what I went through previously, although at the time I was very empty, as it molded me into the person I am today and has given me the perspective to appreciate Jennifer and her true self.

People don't have bad relationships; they simply have relationships.

During one of our early conversations in our coaching relationship, one of my clients was emotionally "stuck" because in his words he wasted six years in his bad relationship. In summary, my reframe was that he had participated in a six-year masters course that taught him what no other course could ever have taught him. He learned what type of woman he really needed to fulfill him. He learned what he didn't want in a relationship, what to watch for and most importantly, how to appreciate the woman he is currently with.

Remember, relationships are intended to create an intimate connection with another person while improving the quality of your life, both emotionally and spiritually. If that is not happening… you need to make some improvements; your partner needs to make some improvements, you both need to make some improvements… or you are not the right people for each other. It happens.

Your World is Not the "Right World" – As we discussed earlier, we all have different models of the world. Our thought process of "what's right" or "how a person supposed to act or do things" is based on our cultural upbringing or our exposure to other people. Thinking we "are right" in how things should be done in a relationship is a natural human experience, yet an inaccurate thought process.

I've been blessed to travel the world sharing my principles on increasing performance through human behavior, and with that, and I've visited over 35 countries. I have met some incredibly good people, and most of those people from other countries have different beliefs about "how" relationships are supposed to operate. Who's right? There is no right. There's just happy and unhappy.

Happiness is the ONLY measurement of success - Through out my 20+ years of studying human behavior, I can tell you with 100% certainty that humans engage in relationships in the pursuit of happiness.

As humans, we have genetic traits to reproduce; yet beyond sustaining human existence on earth, the reason for existence is learning and happiness. For some, it may be the pursuit of happiness.

What do we think will make us happy? Well, that's another story. Some people marry for money, some for looks, some for sex, and others for companionship. Some marry for security, some for acceptance and other marry because they feel they are supposed to.

None of these reasons will make the relationship a work or not work. What makes the relationship work is if you are happy. Sure, we have all seen people stay in relationships, both men and women, for money. Both are unhappy. Their bank accounts may be full, yet they are dying on the inside. Not a fair trade. My motto is **Happiness is the ultimate currency**.

It Takes Two – "It takes two to make a thing go right... it takes two to make it out of sight"... a line from Rob Base's 1988 hit, it takes two. All of us have heard the phrase it takes two, yet to make a relationship work, it takes both parties to participate in personal growth and development. One person could be committed to personal growth and development, yet if the other person is not, the chances of divorce increase each and every year. Human beings have the need to grow. We have the need to improve.

If one person in the relationship is growing and the other isn't, the PWT (Parallel World Theory) gap widens. We find happiness with people who are like us or appreciate us. People can find attraction and a sense of fulfillment early in the relationship with parallel worlds, yet with age, the once parallel worlds often times become unfamiliar over time.

EPILOGUE

T hank you for allowing me to impact your thoughts and hopefully impact your actions.

Wherever you are today, in regards to your business, your career or your relationships, you have the power to make changes in your behavior and change the destiny of your life. We are all hit with challenges throughout the course of our life, yet without challenge there is no growth. Without growth there is no sense of fulfillment.

You can create your own "success wiring" by consistently investing in yourself by reading, listing to watching positive and productive success publications.

The world is changing fast, yet the fundamentals of success remain the same. You have access to all the information you need to make the changes in your psychology and daily actions. Much of my work is available on my youtube channel (Dan Lier) along with many other qualified experts.

In addition, my popular audio programs and books are available on my website at www.DanLier.com

I hope to meet you as the keynote speaker at your company's next event. Until then, keep believing and stay #OnFire.

This is your year to #RiseAbove

ABOUT THE AUTHOR

Dan Lier is a human behavior expert who is a nationally recognized speaker and author. He delivers customized keynote talks focused on Sales, Leadership & Productivity. Dan is the author of four books and has produced and released seven audio programs. His latest CD / audio download release is a seven track compilation titled "Keys to Success – Vol. I"

Over the past 25 years, he has delivered thousands of customized talks to companies, associations and Universities, providing tools and strategies on how to increase performance by changing behavior. His work has been covered by The Today Show, Inside Edition and has been a guest on the O'Reilly Factor and Howard Stern.

Dan is an adjunct professor for the college if business and entrepreneurship at Fort Hays State University in Kansas where he shares his knowledge with future business leaders.

Dan was introduced to human behavior by his college basketball coach Bill Morse who led his team to two successive national basketball championships. Coach Morse sent Dan to a psychologist to improve his rebounding ability. "At 20 years-old going to a psychologist to talk about my internal limitations in regards to rebounding was an interesting experience to say the least," said Lier.

After receiving his bachelor's degree, Dan went on to coach two years of college basketball and received his Masters Degree at Eastern New Mexico University. Dan accepted a job with Federated Insurance, which entailed a 12-month training program. As part of the training curriculum, the trainee's listened to various personal development programs as a class, one of which was an audio book by Dr. Denis Waitley titled "The Psychology of Winning." Dan went on to work with Dr. Denis Waitley for a short period.

In 1994 Dan went to work for Tony Robbins where he was immersed in a unique culture while elevating his speaking and presentation skills. In 2000, Dan left Robbins and pursue began building his speaking and training career.

Dan became the only "success development" personality to consummate a deal with HSN (Home Shopping Network) where Dan made multiple appearances as "America's Coach" and sold thousands of his "10-Minute Coach" audio programs over a two-year period. In 2006, Dan released his first book titled "The 10-Minute Coach – Daily Strategies for Life Success" published by Beaufort Books in New York.

Dan joined the elite faculty at TSTN (The Success and Training Network) with leaders such as Brian Tracy, Les Brown, Zig Ziglar and Denis Waitley where he created 30-minute shows designed for individual and corporate success via subscription.

His passion for psychology continues today as he continues to study psychology, it's history and it's precursors.

Dan Lier continues to speak for companies, conventions and events around the world. His charismatic delivery style, along with his high quality content, provides companies with the tools to increase performance.

Dan lives in Las Vegas with his wife Jennifer and his two children.

IS YOUR CHILD WIRED FOR SUCCESS

As parents, if you knew the environment you are providing your child determines their success or their failure, would you want to know how you could make a difference? Would you want to know how to give your kids the edge?

According to the Psycho-Success Developmental Theory, we are either providing our children with the proper tools for success, or barriers that prevent them from reaching success. Are you a launch pad or a hindrance to your child experiencing success in their life?

What is success you ask? Success is your child having the ability to effectively deal with challenges, obstacles, disappointments and setbacks, and yet through it all, find peace and happiness. Sounds good right? What parent wouldn't want to provide their child with the tools necessary to enjoy a successful life? The challenge is, many parents are focused on ineffective methods, typically because they just don't have the knowledge.

Are you developing a motivated child or a slacker? Yes, you as a parent determine that as well.

Human behavior expert Dan Lier, shares proven research by the most prolific behavioral psychologists in history, along with his Psycho-Success Developmental Theory.

What you will learn:
- How parents set the stage in the Pre-Development Stage
- Developing Respect and a Success Mindset
- Developing the "work-reward" relationship
- Why some kids are motivated and some are not
- How to develop the "Drive for More" or the "Drive to Sustain"
- Why and how kids get "Hard Wired" for success or failure
- Learn how to provide your child with the best chance to succeed in the physical world.

REFERENCES AND CITATIONS

(Endnotes)

1. Bandura, A.; Ross, D.; Ross, S. A. (1961). "Transmission of aggression through the imitation of aggressive models". Journal of Abnormal and Social Psychology **63** (3): 575–582. doi:10.1037/h0045925. PMID 13864605.

2. Ibid

3. Hock, Roger R. (2009). *Forty Studies that Changed Psychology* (6th ed.). Upper Saddle River, NJ: Pearson Education.

4. Ibid

5. Watson, J. B. (1930). Behaviorism (Revised edition). Chicago: University of Chicago Press.

6. Ibid

7. The Little Albert Experiment http://psychology.about.com/od/classicpsychologystudies/a/little-albert-experiment.htm

8. The Great Ideas of Psychology – The Great Courses: The Teaching Company/Audible.com

9. TOLMAN, E C; POSTMAN, L (1954), "Learning.", *Annual review of psychology* **5**: 27–56

10. Hill, Napoleon (1937). Think and Grow Rich. Chicago, Illinois: Combined Registry Company. p. 8. ISBN 1-60506-930-2

11. Why Rich Kids Hate Their Parents – Robert Frank, CNBC http://www.cnbc.com/id/47985781

12. Isaacson, Walter (2012). Steve Jobs (1st Simon & Schuster hardcover ed.). New York: Simon and Schuster. ISBN 978-1-4516-4853-9.

13. "You go, girl" "The Observer Profile: Oprah Winfrey" *The Observer* (UK), November 20, 2005

14. "Oprah Winfrey Interview". Academy of Achievement. January 21, 1991.

15. "Oprah Winfrey". The Biography Channel. Retrieved February 8, 2008.

16. "Before They Were Stars". Msn.careerbuilder.com. January 22, 2010. Retrieved August 26, 2010.

17. Trump: the art of the deal, Paperback, ISBN 978-0-446-35325-0, page 46. "He called his company Elizabeth Trump & Son ..."

63230899R00090

Made in the USA
Lexington, KY
01 May 2017